A Practical Guide to Strategic Narrative Marketing

How to Lead Markets, Stand Apart and Say Something Compelling in a Crowded Content World

Guy Murrel

DENVER, COLORADO

The opinions expressed in this manuscript are solely the opinions of the author and do not represent the opinions or thoughts of the publisher. The author has represented and warranted full ownership and/or legal right to publish all the materials in this book.

A Practical Guide to Strategic Narrative Marketing
How to Lead Markets, Stand Apart and Say Something Compelling in a Crowded Content World

All Rights Reserved.
Copyright © 2016 Guy Murrel
v2.0

This book may not be reproduced, transmitted, or stored in whole or in part by any means, including graphic, electronic, or mechanical without the express written consent of the publisher except in the case of brief quotations embodied in critical articles and reviews.

Outskirts Press, Inc.
http://www.outskirtspress.com

ISBN: 978-1-4787-7757-1

Outskirts Press and the "OP" logo are trademarks belonging to Outskirts Press, Inc.

PRINTED IN THE UNITED STATES OF AMERICA

Introduction:

Does your organization have a voice in shaping the destiny of your industry? Are you providing clarity around the confusion, misperceptions, opportunities and disruption happening all around you?

From startups to Fortune 500 companies, elevating messaging to an industry level is, in our opinion, one of the great missed opportunities in corporate communications today. Not only does it address the need to tell a singular narrative that inspires positive action, it also fuels all forms of marketing – from traditional PR to newer digital and social media programs.

What follows is a new approach we call *Strategic Narrative Marketing*. Use its principles to say something truly meaningful and compelling in your industry. Stand apart and above the competition, influence positive change and use the power of the narrative to align and lead your organization with a common, higher-purpose cause.

Table of Contents

Introduction: iii
Chapter 1
It Started with Category Creation 1
Chapter 2
Strategic Narrative Marketing: An Overview 5
Chapter 3
Enough About You – Mission Statements vs.
Strategic Narratives 8
Chapter 4
Strategic Narratives Guide Strategic Direction 11
Chapter 5
Common Strategic Narrative New Spaces and Themes 14
Chapter 6
Core Tenets and Development Framework for
Strategic Narrative Marketing 23
Chapter 7
Discovery Workshop for Building a Strategic Narrative 26

Chapter 8
    Strategic Narrative Development..................................29
Chapter 9)
    Creating a Strategic Narrative Category or Theme.........32
Chapter 10)
    Creating a Strategic Narrative Statement 34
Chapter 11
    Creating Strategic Narrative Presentation Slides.............37
Chapter 12
    Developing Long-form Category Definition 39
Chapter 13
    Strategic Narrative Marketing Content.........................42
Chapter 14
    Strategic Narrative Marketing in Action 44
Chapter #15
    Conclusion..51

CHAPTER 1
It Started with Category Creation

Some years ago, a local Colorado manufacturer of industrial hardware products came to Catapult with a specific request: *can you help us build a new market category?*

The company had acquired a software platform that automated the gathering and processing of data that had been done manually for decades. The technology was new and disruptive to the market, within an industry that was very "old school" and set in its ways. The main issue, according to the customer: the sales team was struggling to sell its software because an established category did not exist.

The sales team needed to show customers there was a credible market category that supported adopting the technology. And, equally important, make it easier for prospects to sell the concept internally to management and the folks in purchasing. Without a nice "bucket" to categorize the product, sales efforts were bogged down in explaining technical features, how the product worked and other lower-level issues that derailed the sales process. It was a laborious and frustrating *convincing* exercise.

We agreed to take on the project and while prepping for the kickoff strategy session realized we needed to spend most of our time digging into industry dynamics – not talking about the company and product. What were the prevailing trends? What were the perceptions and misperceptions that existed when it came to automation and technology? What were the opportunities – as an industry – to adopt automation software as a means to improve the overall success of the bigger, industry category?

The result was messaging development and the launch of a new category that was based on Lean manufacturing principles. The ensuing launch, including news announcement, detailed white paper and executive briefings with media and analysts, revealed several things to us:

1) We were telling more of a strategic narrative, defining the industry, helping advance it, changing long-held perceptions and shifting away from talking about the company and its product. We were communicating more like industry analysts, and true industry thought leaders.

2) The less the company talked about themselves the better, and the quicker the company was recognized as a software innovator, not just a products company. It was the industry vision that made the company stand out and would make the market take notice.

3) Media and analysts loved it. They were eager to learn, hear the company's vision and feel part of an emerging trend to help their industry.

4) It provided endless topics for thought leadership, including white papers, bylined articles, speaking, blogs, social content and other useful and educational outlets.

5) It attracted support. One of the largest manufacturers in the world loved the idea, and partnered with the client to co-present the new category concept at a major industry conference.

6) It was fun. Defining and launching a new category was exciting and different. Seeing how it was being embraced within the industry was fascinating and rewarding.

7) As marketers, it moved us from convincing to leading.

8) And, finally, it dawned on us that all of our successful clients had <u>one thing in common</u> – *they all were category leaders.*

Since that time Catapult has created a formalized process to help clients develop an industry Strategic Narrative, and create new market spaces as a strategy for leading their industries and attracting support and desired action.

This Guidebook, *Strategic Narrative Marketing*, is our *own* Strategic Narrative Marketing offering. It is our open contribution to the marketing industry. We hope it helps you and your organization, and provides a meaningful contribution to the marketing industry as a whole.

CHAPTER 2
Strategic Narrative Marketing: An Overview

This Guidebook offers a framework for Strategic Narrative Marketing. It is intended to do two things: 1) Shift the way you think about traditional positioning and messaging, and 2) Provide an action path to move from explaining and convincing – to *leading*. It addresses the persistent challenge organizations of all types face in finding something compelling to say as a means to achieving a desired outcome. This can include changing perceptions, swaying influence, increasing brand awareness, building community, driving sales, fundraising, recruiting top talent, being acquired – or just being noticed at all.

Strategic Narrative Marketing provides a clear path of action to create an entirely new market space (category) – one that aims to improve the overall betterment of your industry. It is NOT about you, per se'. As a byproduct, it helps organizations talk about themselves less, and have truly meaningful conversations with all stakeholder groups, from investors, partners and customers to employees, recruits, industry influencers and prospects. More importantly, defining and/or creating a market space is something your entire organization can support, as you all work collectively to build and own it. It creates comradery, instills team spirit and provides a common goal for the whole organization to rally around.

The brand marketing benefits also are significant – as you will create messaging around a new market space, topic or process that is void of any competing organizations, people or messages. This is a powerful proposition today, considering how noisy our markets are and how difficult it is to not only *stand for something*, but to stand apart and above the competition.

With a focus on industry leadership, Strategic Narrative Marketing provides the much-needed fuel to drive all forms of marketing, including advertising, media and analyst relations, and social media and content marketing that require quality, meaningful topics and themes to be effective.

At a deeper level, Strategic Narrative Marketing also can provide transformational benefits to organizations. It can help them not only simplify their "story," but provide a singular message and *purpose* that all stakeholders can believe in, stand behind and evangelize. It provides a purposeful cause that can unify an organization toward a common goal. It is actionable, easy to understand and offers an element of selflessness and inclusiveness that attracts attention and support.

Strategic Narrative Marketing is rooted in public relations, and is the result of Catapult PR-IR, the Boulder-based, b-to-b high-tech agency co-founded in 1999 by myself and Terri Douglas. As a boutique agency, we have spent almost two decades working with small to mid-sized tech firms and startups. In most instances, we are the primary means with which our clients create brand awareness. From the beginning, we always defined our value proposition as: "helping clients achieve market-leading positions." Now, it has shifted to: "helping clients become market *drivers*, not just market leaders."

You too can be a market driver with Strategic Narrative Marketing.

CHAPTER 3
Enough About You – Mission Statements vs. Strategic Narratives

We all know the amount of time and effort that goes into building traditional Mission and Positioning Statements. This soul-searching exercise is played out countless times in business, government, non-profits and educational institutions. White boards are filled with words and statements that define the company, its essence and value proposition.

The problem with Mission Statements, as we see it, is twofold: 1) Most Mission Statements are pretty benign and sound very much alike, and 2) Mission Statements are very inward and often lack a higher level perspective. And, let's be honest, how many times is the mission statement actually used? How does it inspire and encourage actionable participation for the better good, vs. what is typically perceived as a statement that aims to explain and convince?

A Strategic Narrative can help an organization elevate its message much higher than itself, up to the industry level. It demands an organization define its view of the world (industry), what positive change needs to occur, and what role it will play to promote and advance that positive change.

The Strategic Narrative is age-old, as the Romans, Greeks and, of course, the Unites States, all had/have them. In its purest form, it is central to the practice of international relations. Governments use strategic narratives to achieve desired objectives: define their countries' identities, explain their role in the world, identify allies and enemies, establish the nature of the relationships among them and contextualize historical events, as well as create policy decisions.

From Wikipedia: Strategic Narratives provide a "concise statement of what an entity is doing, why and how that links to a positive vision of the future. It outlines the individual actions of members of its own societies and members of other societies whom it wishes to influence."

Each and every organization should adopt a Strategic Narrative to telling its "story." It can and should define the landscape and trends of the industry, and convey a clear vision for the future that focuses on the market segment's growth and promise. This can become your organization's cause and purpose, as the company works to advance the progress and success of its industry. This approach brings a company's vision to life and, as mentioned above, extends beyond marketing to every person in the organization. This also facilitates a single, unified message – a common goal for many organizations that often find it elusive and difficult to create.

CHAPTER 4
Strategic Narratives Guide Strategic Direction

The process of developing a Strategic Narrative can also serve as a forcing function to guide the strategic direction for organizations of all types.

Here are some organizational benefits of Strategic Narrative Marketing:

1) <u>Complacency Safeguard</u>: business as usual is and has always been a killer. The examples of companies that held tight to success models of yesterday and subsequently became irrelevant are numerous. This typically happens when industry and customer behavior mega-trends are ignored or not taken seriously. Following the approach outlined

in this guidebook helps ensure that industry complacency never sets in.

2) Opportunity Creation: purposely exploring industry disruption factors and transformational shifts can uncover new opportunities for growth and competitive advantage. Staying on the leading edge, or even ahead of the industry pack, comes when you commit to taking an active role in leading the advancement of the industry category. This may result in improvements to core offerings, or entirely new opportunities that are developed side-by-side with existing products or services.

3) Competitive Identification: many organizations are fixated on their long-time competitors and fail to recognize emerging ones. Both of these factors can impact all facets of an organization, as well as its long-term success. By identifying emerging mega trends, and the companies that are driving them, you may find new competitors that are worthy of your attention and possible response.

4) Understanding Customer Behavior: customer behavior and brand loyalty are shifting quickly and catching many organizations off-guard. These shifts in customer dynamics range from a new generation of employees replacing an aging workforce and changes in purchasing patterns, to low-cost and mobile app-oriented offerings that potential buyers may find attractive.

Strategic Narratives Guide Strategic Direction

5) <u>Executive Alignment</u>: conducting an industry-focused strategy session (outlined below) often feels like a family holiday dinner when the issues of politics arise – everyone has strongly held and passionately divergent opinions. Most dedicated positioning and messaging sessions focus on what a company does, its value proposition and company differentiation. These are worthy issues to discuss and articulate for sure. However, elevating the discussion to paint a vision for the industry, and the role the organization will play to advance its progress, brings company strategy, or lack thereof, to the forefront. The power of the Strategic Narrative helps resolve these issues and align not only the executive team, but the entire organization.

CHAPTER 5
Common Strategic Narrative New Spaces and Themes

When developing a Strategic Narrative, the end-goal is to create a new market space to message around and champion. Here are some common areas that organizations can focus on when developing a Strategic Narrative:

Create a new industry or product/services category

The process of defining and introducing a new market category can instantly change the way you think about leading your marketing, company and industry. What organization is not facing industry disruption through the rapid pace of change, new competitor entrants and mega-trends involving legislative, technology and behavioral shifts? Perceptions of existing categories are being shattered daily. The global rush of startups all have a single common goal: disrupt every market they enter.

Every organization has the opportunity and right to re-define or create a new market category. Do not leave it up to others to define your industry space!

Organizations that do not adapt and lead are in danger of becoming obsolete and, as it has played out during the past decade or so, vanish all-together. Borders, Blockbuster and AOL are prime examples. All of these organizations failed not only to recognize seismic industry category shifts, but adapt and move to a position of leadership. Looking at Blockbuster, who's to say they couldn't have beaten Netflix to the punch? Maybe they tried, but they were slow to react and failed to re-define their category (video rentals), and before they knew it, they were slipping into failure.

For smaller organizations and startups, defining and promoting a unique and authentic vision for something "new" in the industry, for example a new category or process framework, can be profound. Done right, it rapidly establishes much-needed market credibility, and offers a fresh perspective that is interesting, compelling and action-oriented. From a PR and marketing perspective, it provides a tangible (and audacious) goal. It provides themes for endless fodder and content, and quickly changes the conversation dynamics with influencers and potential customers. It demonstrates true market leadership, and extends an offer to participate in advancing something new and meaningful – which has *less to do with the "nuts and bolts" of what a company actually offers.*

This has been done successfully in the tech and software world, with the creation of the "Agile Manifesto" in 2001. Created by 17 software visionaries during a retreat in Utah, it outlined new principles and core tenets that the software community – as a whole – should take to address the incredible inefficiency and failure rate that plagued the industry at the time. Since then, "Agile" approaches to software delivery are practiced and accepted as mainstream, and adopted by startups and large software organizations alike. It started with a vision for a better performing industry.

Quick Tips:

Make sure the new category, while fresh and new, relates to and addresses issues within an existing category.

- Look to mash-up two existing categories – examples include:
    - Enterprise + Cloud Development
    - Agile + Marketing
    - Millennial + Leadership Development
    - Strategic Narrative + Marketing

> **Quick Tips continued**
>
> ❧ All of the examples above combine two existing, already known concepts. This is important as it makes it easy for people to "get it" on their own without a lengthy explanation.
> ❧ Be ready to define and market it with a vengeance.

Re-define and reinvigorate an existing category

Oftentimes you may operate within a category that is clearly established and defined. However, there is hardly a market space today that is not undergoing continuous change and possible disruption. Identifying trends, challenges and possible contributions to the industry provides an opportunity to share your organization's insights and vision for the future. By defining the landscape and articulating possible solutions to threats at the industry level, not company level, you can align many aspects of your organization around this narrative.

For example, if you work in the financial services industry, what can your industry do to address public concerns and lack of trust, and move forward proactively as a collective community? With the angst against Washington politicians, the U.S. Congress is in desperate need to create a common narrative that accepts ownership of the current situation and, most importantly, outline steps the House and Senate can collectively take to make things better.

The idea here is that "all ships rise with the tide," and your organization has an opportunity to define both the challenges and steps to success for the industry. Evangelizing the category is what true thought leaders and market winners do.

Quick Tips

- ☙ Create an industry "Vision Presentation" that focuses exclusively on industry trends and challenges, and what role your organization will play in advancing the category.
- ☙ Create an "Industry Tenets" bullet sheet that outlines the steps your industry needs to take to move forward and prosper. Turn this into a white paper and other forms of thought leadership content for your company and others to see and adopt in their everyday work activities.
- ☙ Share this industry vision with media and industry analysts, the industry at large (through PR, AR, content and social media marketing) and all stakeholders within your organization.
- ☙ Use the industry narrative to guide product/service development, thought leadership, funding and sales efforts. Gain consensus internally for how each and every person can align goals and objectives with a higher, unified purpose.

Develop a new product or process framework

All industries have certain problems to fix or areas to improve. Consider contributing some of your best thinking to the industry as a means of elevating your company narrative and clearly articulating the leadership role you play within your industry. The software industry has been doing this for years with open source. In fact, some of the most successful tech companies started out sharing and contributing to the overall good of the industry through the open source model (where software is made freely available and is improved by the community itself).

While making a product and giving it away may be prohibitive, think of the unique knowledge that your company has gained during the years and consider if there's something to contribute.

An example is Catapult's client, Amadeus Consulting. This highly successful software consultancy saw a persistent gap in the software development planning process where "business value" was not properly identified and considered when deciding what software features to build. All too often, it saw organizations jump from "ideas to features," without stepping back and asking the right questions during the all-important pre-requirements stage. They knew from experience, that this gap significantly contributed to the high rate of software project failures – *at the industry level.*

As a company, Amadeus developed ID-GEM, a 25-page digital

guidebook to help both techies and business stakeholders communicate better and align project goals. Now the company has shifted from communicating simply what they make and do, to discussing the impact of megatrends like Agile, DevOps, cloud computing, mobile development and the concept that "software is eating the world." They are not only sharing their vision of industry trends – but offering, for free, a solution to the problem/opportunity they identified.

This example not only illustrates how Amadeus is contributing to its industry, but it also distinguishes them as experts through the ID-GEM offering and its industry level narrative about the "planning gap," and the need for business-value upfront planning to reduce the rate of software failures. It is extremely rich and something that is supported by the entire company.

Quick Tips

- Think beyond the common "Top Five Tips" approach of how to do something for thought leadership. Those "tricks and tips" blogs, e-books and articles are still worthy, they just need to support higher Strategic Narrative umbrella messaging that focuses on industry level needs.
- As you brainstorm what type of new industry "contribution" you can offer, involve as many stakeholders as possible to ensure diverse input and cross-departmental support. This strategy is led by marketing and executive leadership, but the core of the knowledge should come from across the organization.

> **Quick Tips continued**
>
> ଓ Be ready to feel uncomfortable, as what you offer will be available to competitors and the industry at large. Resist the urge to make this exclusive and all about marketing. It must be meaningful and authentic.

Educate and/or Clarify a Major Misperception

If creating something entirely new, like a category or process framework, seems too daunting or unrealistic, look for opportunities to create a narrative that helps educate and/or clarify any major misperceptions that can adversely impact your industry. Perhaps it makes the case for new technology over the way a market "has always done things." Perhaps there are misperceptions that are slowing the adoption of products and services in your market segment.

For instance, the cloud computing industry has worked hard to gain the trust of larger enterprise IT organizations. The promise of flexibility and low-cost are well-known. However, if lingering concerns about privacy and security continue, the entire industry will see its growth stall.

Companies that are leading the industry will always play an active role in shaping a positive industry narrative, and proactively and consistently educate the market about the overall benefits, advancements and evolution of the market.

Quick Tips

- If there are major industry roadblocks or challenges, don't hide from them or ignore them. Create a team of people from across the organization to discuss and clarify your organization's opportunity to address the issues in a positive way.
- Take the lead in conducting an industry survey that pinpoints misperceptions and use the results to set a benchmark for the industry to move the needle in the right direction.
- Consider bringing in a well-known industry influencer to collaborate on a narrative for use in a variety of marketing initiatives such as videos, social, content, and PR/ AR activities.
- Always frame your Strategic Narrative as an industry evolution story, and provide clarity on industry perceptions that acknowledge the issues, sets the record straight and outlines steps and progress the industry is making to address them.

CHAPTER 6
Core Tenets and Development Framework for Strategic Narrative Marketing

By now we hope that your mind is busy and starting to percolate ideas for building a Strategic Narrative. Before we get to the steps to build the narrative, we want to share the core tenets of Strategic Narrative Marketing. These tenets are principles you can follow to build and promote your own Strategic Narrative.

7 Core Tenets of Strategic Narrative Marketing:

1. Defines Current Industry Landscape and Trends:

   ❧ The narrative always speaks at the industry level.

2. Paints a Vision for the Future:

   ❧ Outlines the big opportunity for your industry, both short-term and long-term.

3. Serves as Singular Umbrella Message:

   ❧ The narrative rides above all other messaging and serves as a guidepost for what the company stands for in the industry.

4. Becomes a Tangible, Company-wide Initiative:

   ❧ The organization must embrace the industry narrative as a strategic corporate initiative for all stakeholders to support and evangelize – internally and externally.

5. Always Honors the Category

   ❧ The narrative and supporting communications always speak and aim to improve the category – this is a continuous process, not a one-off campaign.

6. Is Open and Inclusive

    ❧ The organization's contributions are always available to all, with adoption of the narrative by competitors considered validation of the approach and a success.

7. Outlines the Company's Role in the industry:

    ❧ Explains where the organization fits in the industry, and how it will contribute to it from an organizational level.

CHAPTER 7
Discovery Workshop for Building a Strategic Narrative

One of the ways we help our client's build their Strategic Narrative is to engage in a Discovery process that gets to the heart of the issues that are at stake. These sessions are of the most insightful, raw, and exciting aspects of building the narrative. We are able to tailor these sessions to suit different cultures to get the best result, but it's important to include a cross-section of executives and employees within your organization to gain a diverse set of perspectives, input and insight. Here is a flow of discovery questions to lead you through a Strategic Narrative Workshop messaging session. Ask and capture input from the following set of questions:

- Industry Dynamics and Trends
  - What is the current state of your industry?
  - What are the megatrends impacting your industry?
  - What are current perceptions and misperceptions concerning your industry?
  - What challenges does your industry face?
- Customer Dynamics
  - How has customer behavior changed in recent years/months?
  - What are the prevailing customer attitudes and hot buttons?
  - How have customer personas changed?
- Industry Vision
  - What is the next big opportunity for your industry?
  - Where do you see your industry one year from now?
  - What new value can your industry deliver to the market?
- Industry Contribution
  - What areas of opportunity or improvement (category, process and product) do you see that would improve your industry?
  - What specifically can your organization offer the industry to make it better?
  - What role will your organization play to improve the industry?

○₈ Benefits
- How will your narrative/contribution benefit:
  - The industry at large
  - End-users and customers
  - Your organization, employees and teams

CHAPTER 8
Strategic Narrative Development

The first step in Strategic Narrative Marketing is the development phase. This effort should be facilitated through a half- or full-day discovery workshop that includes senior management (CEO included), and stakeholders across functions and organizational rank. It is important to invite people who may not be part of the senior management team, yet have experience with product development, sales, support or customer engagement. This is important for two reasons, 1) You want input with a wide range of experience and business touch-points, and 2) You don't want this strictly to be a top-down initiative. You want organizational buy-in and, as is sometimes the case, senior management may be unaware of the realities of what going on "in the trenches."

Use the Discovery Workshop Framework outlined above as

a core template for running your messaging input session: or modify it to include specific issues particular to your industry.

We recommend that the workshop focus exclusively on developing the category and industry-specific topics. The rule during this discussion is simple, but hard for many organizations to abide by: You CANNOT talk about what your company does, its offerings or other "we" statements that steer the conversation downward and inward. The only time the company is discussed is around aspirations of how the organization can contribute to the overall good of the industry. Again, *do not talk about yourselves*!

Also, keep in mind that this is a discovery session only, and – unless it happens organically and with consensus – do not try and "figure it out" and develop the "new space" narrative. A qualified and objective facilitator should ask the questions and lead the discussion. Ideas and thoughts should flow without judgment or editing. All input is good and welcomed. A dedicated note taker should focus exclusively on capturing all input. It also can be a good idea to record the session and have it transcribed.

Narrative Building Tip:

For some, this approach may seem a bit antiquated – so please take this or leave it. However, I like to take a sheet or two of blank white paper and, as I read through the discovery session notes, I jot down key phrases that jump out or I feel are compelling. There will be lots of chatter, but this approach helps me sift through the dialogue, coalesce the "good stuff," and allows me to see recurring themes that inevitably come out of these sessions. I write them out randomly on the blank paper and, as I start to write the narrative based on the framework below, use a highlighter to prioritize and "check off" key themes that have already been written.

CHAPTER 9)
Creating a Strategic Narrative Category or Theme

For those looking to create a new category, as mentioned above, first look at modifying an existing category. This can be done by adding modifiers to an existing category with words like: enterprise, mobile, agile, community, open, dynamic and organic. An example that we created for one of our clients is *Enterprise Mobile Duress*, a call for the security industry to incorporate "people protection" as part of the core areas of enterprise-scale security. Or, think about mashing up two categories. An example of this approach can be seen with the various uses of "Agile," with Agile Marketing and Agile Big Data combining two existing concepts into a singular, new category. Remember, that Strategic Narrative Marketing always requires depth of thinking and content, and the commitment to evangelize and share the opportunities and benefits of a new space. It is not just a tagline to be bantered about.

CHAPTER 10)
Creating a Strategic Narrative Statement

Once you have determined the Strategic Narrative topic, you can start building out the verbiage to support the vision. Similar to the traditional "Positioning Statement" formula, here is a messaging formula for creating a Strategic Narrative Messaging statement. The first section provides the template, followed by a finished statement for Strategic Narrative Marketing.

Creating a Strategic Narrative Statement

Template:

As a member of the _____ industry, COMPANY NAME sees _____ as major mega-trends impacting our industry. We believe the _____ industry has the opportunity to _____ LEADERSHIP ACTION _____ to _____ BENEFIT _____ in the future. To advance our industry, COMPANY NAME offers/pledges to _____ CONTRIBUTION _____ that will help _____ ORGANIZATION + BENEFIT. By supporting _____ CONTRIBUTION _____, COMPANY NAME will help the ___ INDUSTRY BENEFIT ___, ORGANIZATION BENEFIT _____ and INDIVIDUAL BENEFIT.

Finished Strategic Narrative Statement Example:

As a member of the Public Relations industry, Catapult sees the rise of social media and content marketing as major mega-trends impacting our industry. We believe the Public Relations industry has the opportunity to lead the development of strategic messaging and content creation to help organizations communicate more effectively today and in the future. To advance our industry, Catapult offers the Strategic Narrative Marketing framework to help organizations establish new market spaces and industry level messaging that helps differentiate it against competitors, attract meaningful awareness and drive desired business objectives. By supporting Strategic Narrative Marketing, Catapult will help the Public Relations industry maintain ownership of corporate messaging, help customers become market drivers and help PR practitioners assume a more strategic role in their jobs.

CHAPTER 11
Creating Strategic Narrative Presentation Slides

The framework for the Strategic Narrative can be created as a PowerPoint deck that includes, at this point, words, terms and short sentences that make up the narrative. Here's a simple framework to follow:

- Slide #1) Name of new category, process or industry vision statement
    a. Also determine and list key terms and phrases that will be used consistently throughout the narrative. Consistency is imperative!
- Slide #2) Strategic narrative positioning statement (use template above)

- Slides #3- #6) Strategic Narrative outline, with bulleted text on:
  - Slide #3 Title: Industry Mega Trends
    i. define the three major megatrends impacting industry
  - Slide #4 Title: Industry Status
    i. history, current status, disruption factors, challenges, misperceptions and repercussions of the status quo
  - Slide #5 Title: Industry Vision
    i. opportunities, what's needed, new market space or solution, positive impact on industry and action statements that outline what's needed by the industry as a whole to evolve and deliver higher levels of value
  - Slide #6 Title: Company Industry Role
    i. promise to advocate new category/process/vision, role the company will play to advance the industry and new space, action steps it will take to evangelize the new offering, role the company's people and technology will play in advancing the overall industry

CHAPTER 12
Developing Long-form Category Definition

The following messaging approach can be used for creating a category-defining Strategic Narrative in the form of a white paper or positioning paper. Think of these as possible chapter headings and accompanying themes:

History of Category

- When and how was it established?
- What role did the category play when introduced?
- What was the tipping point for growth?

Adoption and Growth

- Once mainstream, how did it grow?
- What factors drove growth or challenges?

- How did the category benefit its professional community?
- How did the category benefit end-users or customers?
- How did the category benefit society?

Pros and Cons

- Three main, global benefits that made/makes the category attractive
- Three main, global reasons people may be turned off by the category

Category Peaks and Valleys

- Times change, how did modernization change or disrupt the category?
- Has the industry landscape undergone drastic or gradual changes (positive or negative)?
- Hard lessons learned – explain any major setbacks the category experienced.
- Was there a single event that propelled or harmed the category? If so, explain.

The Category Today: Is it Still Relevant?

- Current state of the industry/category?
- What are common perceptions and misperceptions?
- How does the category fit or support a larger industry market, society or economy?
- What is the result of staying the course?

Vision for the Category – The Big Opportunity, What Role Can the Category Play?

- What must the category do as a whole to achieve this vision?
- If the category adapts and prospers, what is the big benefit/value proposition?
- What must organizations do to achieve this vision?
- How do you see the category evolving over time, and in what stages, to add greater value for all stakeholders?

CHAPTER 13
Strategic Narrative Marketing Content

Once the core Strategic Narrative is developed, it is time to form the raw narrative into market-facing content. This initial content will serve as the foundation for introducing the new category/market space to the industry. Let's start by creating:

1. White Paper or eBook: this document (possible outline above) adds depth and useful, practical information based on the internal Strategic Narrative messaging. An example of this is the Guidebook you are reading right now. Remember – this document is not about your company or organization, it is an open, inclusive and practical outline of your organization's vision and contribution to the industry.
2. PowerPoint Presentation Deck: having the Strategic Narrative framework and white paper/eBook

completed, now you can port this meaningful information into a presentation deck that can be shared with employees, partners, customers and media and analyst influencers. This can include the slides outlined above, an intro slide on the company and, at the back of the deck, a quick overview of the company offering – and how it supports the new industry contribution.

3. Launch News Release: the PR team can now draft a "launch" news release that announces the new industry category/vision, and the availability of the whitepaper/e-book. This release will be personally shared with media and analyst contacts, and should be issued via one of the leading PR wire services (we use PR Newswire).

4. Corporate Blog Post: this is a more personalized narrative around the "why" and executive vision for the company. It should come from the CEO.

5. Social Media Content: incorporate the new Strategic Narrative and subsequent offering (if available) into all social media programs. This will include pre-launch tweets and graphical content (placards, ads and billboards) for appropriate social channels. Also, for LinkedIn, incorporate short editorial posts that lead back to the whitepaper/eBook.

6. New website re-fresh (or a new website if possible). This will include key homepage messaging and a dedicated section where people can sign-up or just download the narrative document.

CHAPTER 14
Strategic Narrative Marketing in Action

To achieve the value that the Strategic Narrative brings, the outcome needs to be more than a binder of information that sits on the shelf and collects dust. Having a Strategic Narrative in a vacuum is useless and it must be brought to life to reap the benefits. With that, let's focus our attention on the steps or phases needed to develop, launch and evangelize the Strategic Narrative, both internally and externally.

Sidebar: Pre-Phase 1:

Step back and think through some planning issues before diving head-long into rolling out the Strategic Narrative. Start with a straw-man timeline and – most importantly – determine a launch date so this initiative has structure and deadlines. In addition, when planning for the launch, look at possible events or milestones to launch around – a major new product rollout, industry conference or event, or other significant company development.

Phase 1:

Strategic Narrative Launch: Once the Strategic Narrative and supporting content is developed, you can now move toward a major launch campaign to introduce the new messaging and/or framework to the world. As mentioned above, Strategic Narrative Marketing is a PR-centric approach, and the launch concepts outlined here are rooted in PR. That's not to say, by any means, that paid advertisements, social media and content marketing, paid search and sponsored campaigns should be excluded. Of course, the more firepower the better! However, at a bare minimum, good solid PR strategies and tactics need to be executed to both introduce and build awareness and credibility. Good PR is still the most authentic and impactful way to create meaningful brand awareness, and to shift industry perceptions.

Launch Framework:

1. Select a launch date: this is the day the new narrative/offering will be introduced into the market. All activities work back from this date, and all activities – PR, AR, social, content, website should all "activate" on this day. You want to punch hard into the market.
2. Content development: as outlined above: news release, white paper/e-Book, PowerPoint presentation and

blog/social content. All prepped and ready to go on launch date, and, in the case of pre-briefings and pitching, prior to launch date (usually news release and PPT at a minimum).
3. Rollout internally: not too far in advance, but make sure the entire organization has been introduced to the new narrative, preferably through an all-hands meeting. Remember, this is a company-wide initiative. This is an important element and one that should not be overlooked.
4. Pre-pitching: follow the classic product launch process of pre-briefing media and analysts prior to the launch date. Work to get as much coverage to hit on the launch date as possible.
5. Social media campaigns: prepare all Twitter, Facebook and LinkedIn (and other applicable platforms) to go live on the launch date. Include organic and paid campaigns.
6. Content marketing: prepare blogs and possible by-lined articles (and perhaps an op-ed piece) to go live on launch date.
7. Website re-fresh: incorporate the new narrative/offering on the website. The white paper/e-Book can serve as a lead generator by asking for name and email sign-up.
8. Launch Day: on the pre-determined launch date, all of the above listed steps should go live.
    a. New release hits the wire

b. Email to all partners and customers

   c. Social and content goes live

   d. Monitor and respond to social to increase buzz and engagement

Phase 2

<u>Strategic Narrative Evangelization:</u> Now that the Strategic Narrative has been launched – there is still much work to be done. You do not want to launch the narrative and go quiet for the next couple of months. Because this is "new" industry messaging and concepts, you will need to assume leadership in evangelizing the narrative. The PR/marketing team needs to create an action plan for follow-up strategies and tactics that promote the category and company vision.

Circle the marketing wagons around the narrative/category to promote and evangelize through ongoing campaigns and tactics.

1. Media relations
    a. Evergreen pitching, news announcements, interviews/ briefings on the narrative and market category, inclusion in round-up stories (these are usually focused on industry trends anyway) and op-ed pieces

2. Analyst relations
    a. Always use the narrative as part of every briefing, brief analysts on a regular basis on the maturity of the space, work to influence the influencers, and promote the use of the narrative as part of the industry dialog and research report content and structure

3. Content marketing
    a. Create an ongoing editorial calendar of topics surrounding the narrative for blogs and by-lined articles, tie to business, vertical industry and local markets. Make content readily available and as a means of keeping the narrative fresh and "out there"

4. Social media marketing
    a. Embed the narrative, and promote the associated content, via the social media channels that are most relevant for your company and target audience(s). Look to create new Twitter handles and LinkedIn groups that are focused exclusively on the narrative topic/offering

5. Speaking and Awards
    a. Use the narrative as the foundation for speaking abstracts and as the primary theme to evangelize at industry events. Identify and submit for awards that can support the narrative. As

these opportunities are secured, promote via content and social media

6. Events
    a. Look to host and attend engaging events that support the Strategic Narrative. This can include: webinars, MeetUps, user groups, roadshows and conference sponsorships
7. Internal Communications
    a. Solicit internal support for evangelizing the new narrative/category. Encourage social media amplification, speaking at events, blogging and other forms of communication support. Also share progress and developments with how the Strategic Narrative is taking hold in the industry

Also consider third-party influencers (beyond media and analysts), to help promote the narrative within the industry. This can include partners, customers and employees.

The bottom-line is you and your organization will need to push the narrative consistently and with passion!

Phase 3

Strategic Narrative Industry Adoption: After three to six months of evangelizing the Strategic Narrative the next wave of effort should focus on industry adoption. If it hasn't already happened (at least from competitors), additional third-party support needs to be incorporated into the evangelize phase (this never stops). This can include:

1. Customer testimonials
    a. Case studies
    b. Webinars
    c. Joint speaking
2. Working to get the category included in research analyst reports, or as a track at an industry event
3. Op-ed articles from key editors and/or bloggers
4. In-person event – this could be a local MeetUp, user group conference of sponsored event at an industry conference.

The idea here is to move beyond self-evangelizing to gaining the support of key third-party influencers. If this is prohibitive, keep the drumbeat going and think of it as a political campaign – hammer on the issue with an aim to own the category!

CHAPTER #15
Conclusion

Creating something new and compelling to say is a goal of most organizations – as a means to differentiate, attract customers and create a market position that is tops in the industry. Industry and category leaders are the ones that are always short-listed, sought out by media and analysts, raise the most money and stay one step ahead of the competition.

We hope that this new marketing framework – based on the core tenets of the Strategic Narrative – will help you think bigger, reach higher and lead your organization to new heights.

www.ingramcontent.com/pod-product-compliance
Lightning Source LLC
Chambersburg PA
CBHW021040180526
45163CB00005B/2217